A HELPING HAND

ROMAN AND IRIS

Quarto is the authority on a wide range of topics.

Quarto educates, entertains and enriches the lives of our readers—enthusiasts and lovers of hands-on living.

www.quartoknows.com

Author: Nancy Loewen
Illustrator: Elisa Paganelli
Editors: Ellie Brough and Victoria Garrard
Designer: Victoria Kimonidou
Consultant: Joanna Silver

© 2020 Quarto Publishing plc

This edition first published in 2020 by QED Publishing,
an imprint of The Quarto Group.
The Old Brewery, 6 Blundell Street,
London N7 9BH, United Kingdom.
T (0)20 7700 6700 F (0)20 7700 8066
www.QuartoKnows.com

A catalogue record for this book is available from the British Library.

ISBN 978 0 7112 5097 0

9 8 7 6 5 4 3 2 1

Manufactured in Guangdong, China TT032020

MIX
Paper from
responsible sources
FSC® C016973
FSC
www.fsc.org

All web addresses included at the back of this book were correct at the time of printing. The publisher cannot be held responsible for the content of the websites referred to in this book.

ROMAN AND IRIS

A story about bullying

BY

NANCY LOEWEN

ART BY

ELISA PAGANELLI

Roman flung off his covers. He wolfed down his breakfast. He couldn't wait to go to Camp Kinetic, his summer day camp.

In the morning he played parachute games and made galaxy slime.

In the afternoon he drove a go-kart. Camp Kinetic was so much fun!

Then something happened.

At snack time, Roman accidentally bumped into Iris. Her biscuits fell to the ground.

"Watch out, dummy!" she said loudly. She grabbed Roman's biscuits and stomped off.

Later, at story time,
Iris stared at him.

Roman didn't like the
way it made him feel.

Every day, Iris found a new way to trouble Roman.

She tripped him up.

She took his
water at lunch.

She bumped
into him... hard.

But no one seemed to notice.

Roman didn't fling off his covers anymore. He didn't wolf down his breakfast. His stomach hurt too much.

"What's the matter?" his mum asked. "I thought you loved Camp Kinetic."

Roman shrugged. He didn't say anything about Iris. He wanted to. But he didn't.

That day in Art, Iris took the dragonfly
stamp right out of his hands.

"Hey!" said the girl sitting
next to him. Her name was
Hazel. "Mr Wells, Iris took
Roman's stamp!"

"Just kidding," Iris said.
She gave the stamp back.

Camp Rules

Mr Wells spoke
to Iris quietly.

He pointed to the
camp expectations
posted on the wall.

Iris didn't take Roman's water at lunch.
She didn't trip him. But whenever Roman
looked up, she was staring at him.

"Just ignore her,"
Hazel told Roman.

But Roman didn't know
how to do that.

That night Roman asked his mum if he could quit Camp Kinetic.

"Tell me what's happening," she insisted. "I'm your mum. It's my job to listen."

So Roman finally told her about Iris.

Together they decided that they would
talk to the camp director in the morning.
Just telling his mum made him feel a
tiny bit better. No, a LOT better.

At bedtime, his mum read him an extra story
and gave him an extra-long cuddle.

The next morning, Roman and his mum told Mrs Franklin about how Iris had been treating Roman.

"I'm glad you spoke up," Mrs Franklin said to Roman. "Camp is for learning and having fun. You can't do that if someone is being mean to you. And it doesn't sound like Iris is very happy, either. We'll do our best to help both of you."

From then on, the camp leaders watched Iris and Roman closely. They made sure Roman wasn't bothered and they talked to Iris about her behaviour.

Over the next few days, Roman's stomach stopped hurting so much. If Iris stared at him, he took a deep breath and told himself to ignore her. Pretty soon she hardly looked at him at all.

Roman found camp fun again. And Iris seemed happier too.

Every morning Roman flung off his covers.
He wolfed down his breakfast.

He was going to have a great day!

NEXT STEPS

We hear a lot of talk about bullying these days. But what is it, exactly?

 ### What is bullying?

Bullying is repeated behaviour that is intended to harm someone else. It can take many forms: taunting, name-calling, hitting, tripping, pushing and taking or breaking a person's things. Bullying can also include anti-social behaviours, such as spreading rumours or leaving someone out on purpose. Threats and intimidation can be considered bullying as well.

 ### Where does bullying happen?

Bullying can happen anywhere: at school, on the bus, on the playground, even in your own home or neighbourhood. Children who bully come in all shapes and sizes, and bullying can happen one-on-one or in groups.

 ### What effect can bullying have?

It's important to realise that bullying is NOT a normal part of childhood. It can have serious long-term consequences. Children who are bullied may struggle to learn new things. They may be more likely to develop depression and anxiety. And the children who are doing the bullying may need help as much as their victims do — as adults, they are far more likely to end up in the criminal justice system. In short, bullying isn't a matter of 'kids being kids'. Bullying is a serious public health problem. It's up to all of us to create an environment in which all types of bullying behaviour are considered unacceptable.

 ### What can you do?

You might think you'll know if your child is being bullied, but often children will keep it to themselves. They might feel ashamed or powerless and don't want you to think less of them. If you notice any changes in your child's behaviour like the ones listed on this page, talk to your child and try to work out the cause.

SIGNS THAT A CHILD IS BEING BULLIED

- Uncharacteristically quiet or withdrawn
- Lack of enthusiasm about school or other activities
- A drop in academic performance
- Tearfulness
- Heightened anxiety
- Changes in eating habits (a lack of appetite or overeating)
- Unexplained bruises
- Bed wetting
- Acting in bullying ways towards others

HOW TO HELP

How can you help your child if he or she is being bullied?

Listen

First, listen calmly. Praise your child for talking to you, and do your best to keep communication going. Reassure them that they are not to blame, and that things will get better.

Role play

Sometimes a child who bullies will back down if given enough pushback. Help your child develop the confidence to stand up to a bully. Role play can be an effective way to do this. Come up with scenarios and practise what to say and do. Using toys to act out scenarios can make your child feel more comfortable. Another strategy is to teach your child deep breathing or other relaxation techniques. Being able to stay calm will give your child a greater sense of control.

Ask for help

While instilling a sense of confidence and self-reliance in a child is always a good idea, it's not fair or realistic to expect children to solve all bullying problems on their own. Your child is not to blame – the problem is the behaviour of the child who is bullying. Report the behaviour to teachers, bus drivers, parents or other adults. Make sure your child knows that this is not a sign of weakness. It's a responsible choice. We need to do all we can to make bullying socially unacceptable.

Support

Finally, give your child extra reassurance and support. Let them know that they are not alone. You will be there for them, no matter what.

IS YOUR CHILD BULLYING OTHERS?

What can you do to turn things around?

 ### Talk and listen
You might feel angry if you find out your child has been bullying others, but it's important to stay calm. Talk to your child and find out why they have been behaving this way. Your child needs to feel supported, but at the same time they need to know that bullying is unacceptable.

 ### Work with the school
If the bullying occurs at school, stay in touch with your child's teachers. It's natural to feel embarrassed, but don't be put off. Educators have lots of experience dealing with all sorts of behaviours, and they can support both you and your child.

 ### Teach social and emotional skills
Show your child what healthy relationships look like and give lots of positive reinforcement when their behaviour improves. If your child continues to bully, consider getting them a mental health evaluation. Addressing these issues when your child is young is an act of kindness and love.

FURTHER RESOURCES

www.bullying.co.uk
Part of the charity Family Lives, this website provides information, support and helplines for children, and their parents, experiencing bullying.

www.childline.org.uk/ info-advice/ bullying-abuse-safety
This charity provides valuable information on bullying and safe forums for discussing situations and finding help.